Inside cover pages. A swarm of locusts over Dubai in 1953.

— DUBAI —

AN ARABIAN
— ALBUM —

Public celebrations beneath Bury Khalifa, on the edge of Shindaga.

DUBAI

AN ARABIAN ALBUM

BY
RONALD CODRAI

MOTIVATE
PUBLISHING

Published by
Motivate Publishing

P.O. Box 2331
Dubai, UAE

P.O.Box 43072
Abu Dhabi, UAE

London House,
26/40 Kensington High Street
London W8 4PF

Directors:
Obaid Humaid Al Tayer
Ian Fairservice

Edited by:
Ian Fairservice
Julia Roles

First published July 1992
Reprinted December 1992

British Library Cataloguing-in-Publication Data.
A catalogue record for this book is available from the
British Library.

ISBN 1 873544 27 8

Colour-separated, printed and bound in the
United Arab Emirates by Emirates Printing Press, Dubai.

CONTENTS

INTRODUCTION 8

ARRIVING IN DUBAI 16

RECOLLECTIONS OF OLD DUBAI 36

DUBAI AT MID-CENTURY 52

AL AKUS 212

GLOSSARY AND NOTES 218

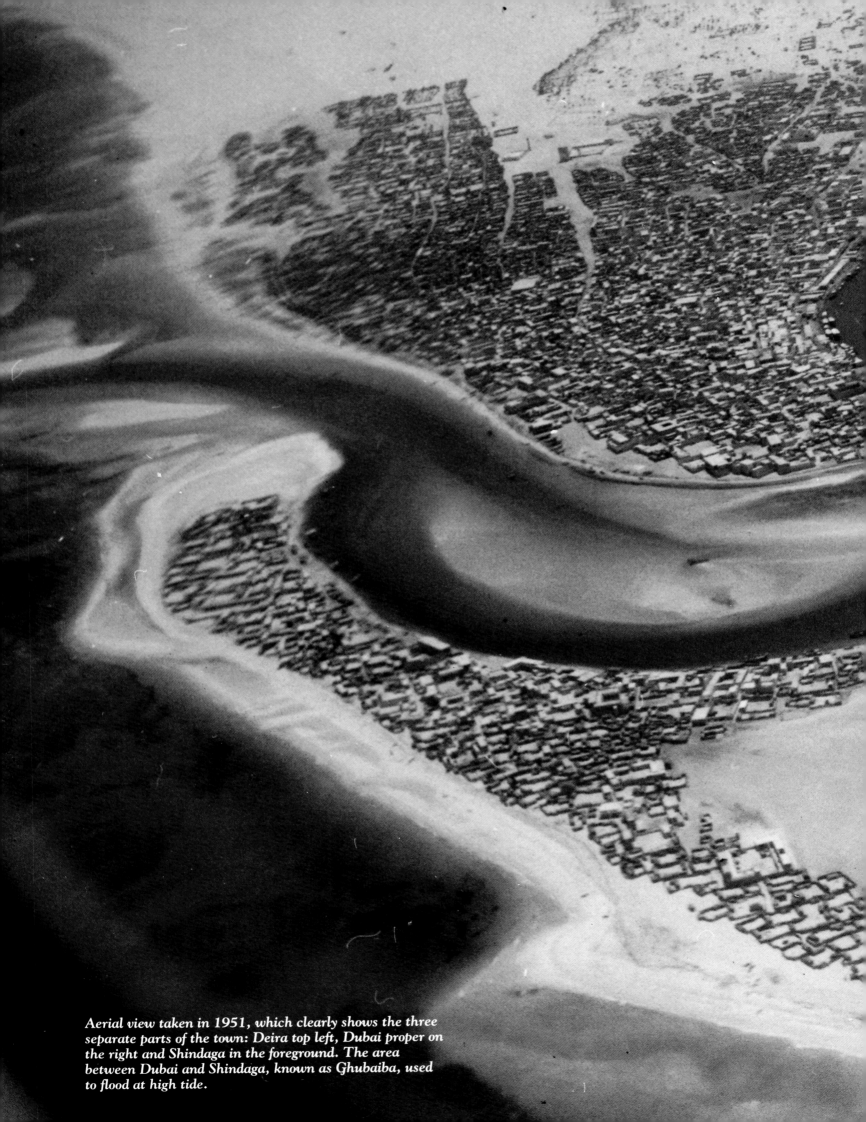

Aerial view taken in 1951, which clearly shows the three separate parts of the town: Deira top left, Dubai proper on the right and Shindaga in the foreground. The area between Dubai and Shindaga, known as Ghubaiba, used to flood at high tide.

Returning to Jumaira on foot after a visit to Dubai suq.

INTRODUCTION

venture through the channel when the sea was rough, for the sand at the entrance to the creek was constantly on the move and the course of the channel might have changed during the sailor's absence on a single voyage.

"Al hamdu' lillah," muttered Saif and several members of the crew as the channel opened out into the still, deep waters of the creek. Arriving from the open sea which had been heavily pounding our vessel, into the dead calm and sheltered waters of Dubai creek, gave rise to a rather curious tranquillity, rather like when the engines of an aircraft are finally switched off after a long flight. Tension, discomfort and tiredness suddenly gave way to frivolity. Some hurried grooming led to a few ribald remarks and, on my part, a renewed curiosity about the town that sat on both sides of the winding bend of the creek.

There were sandbanks inside the creek, of which Al Hadd was the largest, Saif explained, but they presented no problems to anyone who knew Dubai, as they did not change position and there was deep water right to the end of the ten-mile-long inlet. As we followed the deep channel that hugged the shore of Shindaga, he pointed out various landmarks to me, mostly the houses of shaikhs and a few prominent merchants, including the Ruler's winter home. We were close enough for him to shout greetings to people on the bank, people whom I was also to get to know in the years that followed.

Arriving by sea was a good way of appreciating the natural, geographical advantages that accounted for Dubai's success as the leading entrepot in the southern part of the Gulf — namely its large deep-water inlet (albeit with its precarious entrance), access to the interior, and a subterranean supply of sweet water which could be tapped through shallow, man-dug wells. The presence of such water was usually indicated by palm trees, planted and irrigated by the inhabitants of sprawling settlements such as Jumaira. Most of all, the successful exploitation of such natural advantages, and the creation of a thriving trading centre, were the results of the enterprise of its inhabitants.

My arrival was by a local craft but another way of arriving by sea was by mail steamer. Since the beginning of the century, steamers of the British India Steam Navigation Company had called at Dubai every two weeks on their way up the Gulf from Bombay, and every two weeks on their return. The Ups and the Downers (Maaley and Sanaan), as they became known locally, would anchor at a safe distance from the shore, from where they would load and discharge goods ferried by local lighters. If it was very rough, passengers and goods would be carried on to the next port of call, a great disappointment to us when we were expecting mail or some small luxury.

Right. Arriving by sea, with the buildings of Shindaga in the background.

Below. The presence of subterranean water was usually indicated by palm trees which were planted and tended by the inhabitants of sprawling settlements such as Jumaira.

From the desert

Not even campers with the experience of bedu could have lit a fire and prepared food or coffee in the sand-laden wind which had been blowing all day. Our dinner consisted of some rather old tamr (pressed dates) and fresh camel's milk, the froth on which the wind kept trying to blow away, covering it with sand in the process. We had hoped to reach Dubai by nightfall and have a good meal, but although it was only a couple of hours ride away we were all tired, and Abdulla bin Husain said it would be unwise to arrive after dark as the guards in the watchtowers would be trigger-happy as a result of the current insecurity in the area, particularly as the suhail (the dry wind from the south) made everyone rather nervous.

Without the comfort of the coffee-pot we retired early, but it was a disturbed night, and I alternated between pulling my blanket over my head to keep off the stinging, irritating sand, and lowering it to get cooler air. Our camels spent the night snorting and groaning, though whether in protest at the wind or at being hobbled was not clear.

Towards dawn the wind dropped, and I fell into a deep sleep, but it was short-lived as my companions, awake for their dawn prayers, were loudly greeting and wishing each other a good morning as if they had just met, and I was not excluded. It mattered little, for the first fly had arrived, against which the blanket once again proved unsatisfactory protection. As on the previous days of the trip, I was stiff from riding all day, and became a reluctant early-riser, to be greeted with hot coffee, served in several tiny quantities in succession by Ahmed who stood over me with the pot as I sipped. Meanwhile, Obaid was busy making a dough from flour, sugar and water which he shaped into small patties and cooked on the embers of the small fire on which the coffee pot stood regally. We ate and drank with relish, finishing the dates and drinking more warm camel's milk, with some thought of the better fare that awaited us when we reached Dubai.

As we were loading the camels, a party of bedu arrived. Abdulla was highly apprehensive as they approached, for he had identified them as Awamir, but when they drew closer he recognised one of them, and all was well. Abdulla came originally from Ajman, but had long-since moved to Dubai where he was one of Shaikh Rashid's closest and most trusted companions, and was as concerned as his Shaikh at maintaining a good relationship with neighbouring tribes, even when they had as bad a reputation for ghazu as the Awamir.

"Shu al ulum?" ("What is the news/knowledge?") he asked the visitors after the customary greetings and how-do-you-do's.

"None, the world is resting," they replied.

Right. A camel being milked in the desert. Dried dates and camel's milk were the bedu's staple diet.

Below. A group of bedu sitting on top of a dune, keeping their heads slightly above the stinging, suffocating sand being lifted by a strong wind.

But after coffee their news began to trickle out. Tuwairish the bandit had again been active in the area, someone had stolen someone else's camels, a rumour that the price of rice had soared, and the deposed Ruler of Ras Al Khaimah was still holding out in Hawailat from where he exercised control over Wadi Al Qor and had imposed a toll on travellers. Abdulla told me that they were glad they had met him, for they could now travel under his auspices to Dubai where they proposed to offer their support to the shaikhs, the usual ploy when bedu were seeking presents of money in return for their possible support in times of need.

We were now an impressively sized party of nearly twenty, with more than that number of camels, as we started the last lap of our journey. Our arrival in Dubai would no doubt cause more than a little consternation until we were close enough to the watchtowers to be identified. By this time I had become accustomed to riding Omani style, perched somewhat precariously on the camel's rump with legs draped over flopping goatskins of water. The damp, squelching skins tended to make my legs sore, so I tried squatting on my legs bedu style, but that was even more precarious and far from comfortable. We rode in single file on a track which had been erased by the wind from soft sand but which was still visible in sheltered hollows and on sabkha (salt marshes). When riders rode two abreast they left behind what might have been car tracks, the two single camel tracks being spaced about the same distance apart as car wheels.

On the approaches to Dubai, bedu had to decide whether to leave their camels grazing on the sands or whether to take them into town and hobble them conveniently at hand on some open piece of land, though without grazing. Much depended on the expected duration of their stay and whether they would be loading goods on them. Our camels all belonged to Shaikh Rashid and we would ride them into town, after which a bedu lad would take them back into the desert to graze until they were again required. Zeina might be kept behind for her milk, in which case she would be fed on bundles of fodder which could be bought in the suq, but which were expensive.

The sight of palm trees indicated that we were nearing town. On the outskirts of Dubai, they were dotted about the sands rather than in groves, and through them was a long thin strip of habitation. Apart from the windtowers, little of the town was high enough to be visible from a distance. Merged with the palm trees were clusters of the barastis (huts made from palm fronds) in which about two-thirds of the population of around 15,000 lived. We arrived at a watchtower and its guard leaned over its crenellations for a noisy exchange of greetings and news with Abdulla.

"Have you taken prisoners?" he called.

Right. "After coffee their news began to trickle out."

Below. A bedu en route to Dubai through the palm trees which were dotted about on the outskirts of the town.

"If we had, would we have left them with their rifles?" came the sharp response from Abdulla, pointing at the Awamir.

We passed a young boy shepherding a large flock of goats out to the sands. With the approach of summer, each day he had to go further in his search for grazing. Abdulla explained that people in town usually owned only one to three goats, and would pay a boy a small sum every month to graze them. Every morning they would push their animals out of their barastis to join a flock being gathered and led by the boy calling, clucking and hooting at them. In the evening, the returning flock would slowly disintegrate as each goat broke away to return to the barasti where it belonged.

After the warm but keenly dry suhail that had been blowing, the high humidity of the coast suddenly hit us like a wet cloth, and it felt hot and clammy although in fact the temperature was lower. Suddenly we were riding between houses and, as we encountered more and more people going about their daily tasks and bustling to and from the suq (market), we dismounted and led our camels. Only people of tribal origin seemed to pause and appraise us. Abdulla was so well-known that it struck me that he could have led a whole army of invaders into town without anyone doubting his intentions.

From the air

Although Dubai was little-known outside of the region, and even in most parts of the Arab world, there was one rather anomalous way in which it had appeared on the map of progress. At mid-century, civil air travel was on a minor scale, and although rapidly expanding after World War II, the era of mass travel by air as we know it today was barely in its infancy. At that time, aircraft had much shorter flight durations, so the main air routes were dotted with refuelling or staging posts and emergency landing strips. Some were in far-flung places, taking their names from settlements which were sometimes little more than clusters of huts, to which fuel had to be transported on pack animals. More conveniently situated were buoyed channels where flying boats landed, such as in Dubai's creek which, since 1937, had been used on the air route from Britain to India.

Barely conscious that they were in a remote part of Arabia, passengers were ferried ashore and taken under escort (the Rulers of Dubai and Sharjah having entered into a joint agreement undertaking responsibility for their safe conduct) to spend the night in a fort built by Imperial Airways (the forerunner of British Airways) beside the landing strip in Sharjah. Their aircraft was refuelled from four-gallon tins of fuel transported by local craft from the nearest oil refinery at Abadan, at

Right. A Rapide flying west over Shindaga in 1949. The nearest serviceable landing strip was at the R.A.F. staging post at Sharjah. A rare photograph, included for its subject interest rather than its photographic quality.

Below. A barasti coffee shop, which opened around 1950, on the tip of Dubai to which people would cross from Shindaga (shown in the background).

the head of the Gulf. The journey from London to Bombay took several days and entailed many refuelling stops. It is probable that the passengers were as little affected by the experience as were the people of Dubai, once they had become accustomed to the spectacle of the giant, noisy "English Duck" landing in their creek. The buoys marking the channel in Dubai's creek were lifted in 1947, but some years later I witnessed the unheralded arrival and landing in the creek of a chartered flying boat which, according to local gossip, was laden with gold!

There was no shortage of land in and around Dubai, so it was not surprising to find that the town had a long, low profile which seldom rose higher than its palm trees, or the masts of large sailing vessels moored in its creek. Its highest points were on its watchtowers and distinctive windtowers, and atop Fahidi Fort. Even so, those vantage points were not high enough to show the layout and extent of the town, so I was fortunate to have the opportunity to take a few photographs from the air. I believe it is these, more than any others in my collection, which now serve to demonstrate the full extent of the massive, man-made developments which have changed the town so dramatically. They show that even the shape of its coastline has been altered by dredging and reclamation, which is a far cry from the days when the only changes in physical features were brought about by the constant movements of tides and currents stirring the sand from its rest, and by winds that caused the dunes to creep forward at an imperceptible pace, yet enough to menace carefully nurtured palm trees.

Seen from the air, Dubai's creek was, beyond doubt, the town's principal feature. Separating the three well-defined segments of the town, its calm waters provided sheltered anchorage on a coastline exposed to the full force of the shamal which, all too often, lashed at Dubai's windward shores.

From above, the land took on as many hues as the shallow sea that lapped at its edges, particularly where water seeped up through low-lying sand and sabkha. Thin lines of camel trails, areas around wells, and footpaths that converged on the market place were all darkened by constant use. White single- or two-storied houses built of gypsum and coralstone stood out prominently from the large clusters of barasti huts with their compounds which surrounded them and which tended to exaggerate the size of the built-up area. Many palm trees, the principal source of the material for the barastis, dotted the sands around the town.

Very little of the town, as shown in the photographs I took from the air, has survived the widespread changes that have since occurred, except where preserved and cherished as historical heritage.

Right. Aerial view across the creek to Deira, taken in 1951.

Below. A guard in one of the constantly manned turrets of Fahidi Fort. A chandal served as a flagpole, under which a shelter had been improvised from chandals and palm fronds.

The finish of a camel race near the Ruler's house in Shindaga.

RECOLLECTIONS OF OLD DUBAI

Three towns in one

The coastal town of Dubai was divided by water into three distinct parts: Deira, on the east bank of the creek; Shindaga, occupying a spur of land separating the creek from the sea; and Dubai proper (from which the whole town took its name) on the western side. Each sector of the town had its own character. Deira was the largest, and the main commercial part of the town and, being on the right side of the creek, it had the easiest route to Sharjah and the northern Shaikhdoms. From Dubai and Shindaga, Deira could only be reached by boat or by a difficult detour of over twenty miles around the whole of the creek.

The smallest sector of the town was Shindaga, a narrow neck of land bounded on one side by the sea and on the other by the creek. It was separated from Dubai proper by a wide stretch of level sand called Ghubaiba, over which the waters of the creek would flood at high tide. Having no suq of its own, Shindaga was the quietest, mainly residential, part of town, and during the day a steady trickle of people walked back and forth to the suq in Dubai, at high tide carrying their sandals and pulling up their long clothes to paddle through the water.

Although Dubai as a whole was the cosmopolitan home to people of various nationalities, the residents of Shindaga were mostly Arabs of tribal origin, with their many retainers and servants of African blood. Its special character stemmed from the fact that it was the principal and traditional home of Dubai's ruling shaikhs. It was also the site of the Ruler's winter majlis (court or sitting place), which meant that visitors were constantly coming and going. Merchants arrived on foot from Dubai and by abra (ferryboat) from Deira. Bedu came on their camels which they left hobbled wherever there was space, and access to the majlis was sometimes through a disorderly, noisy gaggle of their parked beasts. Some bedu would leave their camels grazing in the desert then, having left behind their means of subsistence, would attach themselves to the Ruler's retinue of armed tribesmen and thus become one of the Ruler's guests. Receiving visiting bedu was an important part of the process by which the Ruler maintained his influence in tribal areas, and bedu would be treated and given presents according to their standing and the political needs of the day. Staunchly independent, bedu expected ease of access to a shaikh's majlis, where they would address him by name without a title, as they would each other. Life in the majlis was a microcosm of life in both desert and town, and was very open. I always enjoyed my frequent visits to the Ruler's majlis, and to the homes of the ruling shaikhs, for they were exceedingly hospitable and treated me as a close friend.

Right. Ibrahim Lootah, a trusted retainer of the Ruler of Dubai. Family retainers were usually of African blood whereas armed guards were of tribal origin.

Below. High tide over Ghubaiba. Ladies wade through the water as they return home to Shindaga from Dubai.

Gypsum, chandals and coralstone

The majority of the population lived in huts made mostly from the fronds of palm trees, but some lived in houses which, like forts and watchtowers, were built of locally available gypsum and coralstone (the "bricks and mortar" of the Shaikhdoms) with their roofs supported by mangrove poles from Africa.

Most of the year the bedu of south-eastern Arabia were able to live in the open, making only occasional use of small, improvised tents and shelters, although some had families living in barasti huts in or near settlements. Their lifestyle was different from that of the bedu of other areas who lived in large, woollen tents — the famous black tents of Arabia.

Locally, it was the huts made of palm fronds which were called tents (khiyam), though they were also called arish and barasti, the latter being one of those words of unknown origin like dhow which English speakers thought was Arabic and the Arabs thought was English.

These "tents" made highly satisfactory dwellings for the settled or semi-settled people of the Shaikhdoms. They had a soft, clean floor of sand, provided good shade and were well-ventilated by any movement of air, without loss of privacy. The occasional rain was welcomed as a blessing, even when, on rare occasions, it leaked into the huts, though hasir mats were sometimes fixed over the fronds of the roof to provide extra protection against the elements. Fences of fronds were often built around one or more huts, creating a useful enclosure for a family unit, in which their livestock could be kept at night.

Stone houses, watchtowers, parts of the suq and even forts could be built mainly of material available locally. Coralstone could be lifted from the shallow waters of the creek, but also from the sea. Gypsum (juss) was dug out of the salt marshes at the end of the creek and fired or baked as required, usually near where it was to be used. Although split palm trunks could, with difficulty, be used as rafters, mangrove poles (chandals) imported from Africa were more durable and more widely used. However, being on average little more than ten to twelve feet long, this greatly restricted the size of rooms and verandas. The only way that a room could be widened was to strengthen its walls and use them to support a heavy teak beam (perhaps cut from the old mast of a ship), on either side of which lines of chandals could be arranged. The rafters would then be covered with hasir mats and gypsum. One of few examples of this was in the Ruler's winter majlis in Shindaga. Subject to cost and availability, a foundation of cement would do much to lengthen the life of buildings,

Right. Some of the teak beams used in the construction of the larger buildings were cut from the masts of ships.

Below. A bedu with his saluki beside an improvised tent of palm fronds, hasir matting and woollen cloth. Unlike the sturdier barasti huts used as dwellings, this was only a temporary shelter.

particularly near the creek and sea where there was a salt-water seepage near to the surface. Imported wood, either soft wood from packing cases or teak from the boat-builder's yard, was used to make doors, window frames and shutters. Iron bars were spaced across the windows, over which crudely made wooden shutters would be closed when there was a storm or a hot southerly wind blowing, or in an effort to keep out wind-blown sand. Glass was never used in windows.

Forts, watchtowers and windtowers, constructed with coralstone, gypsum and chandals, were reinforced in places with blocks of sandstone, or with cement when it was available, but it had to be imported and so was expensive. Like the boat builders, house builders seldom used plans, working mainly by rule-of-thumb, using skills and traditional designs they had learned during long apprenticeships with their fathers.

One of the noticeable features of buildings was the protrusion from them of the unused ends of chandals. The chandals would never be cut flush with the building as they would outlast the building itself and would have a resale value long after the building had crumbled. Hacked out of mangrove swamps in east Africa, chandals constituted one of the main non-edible imports. They were put to many uses but mainly as the framework of the better-made barasti houses, and as rafters of stone buildings.

As was the case with most of the houses built near the creek or the sea, the house in which I lived was very damp as a result of an upward seepage from its base, as well as from the very high humidity. For this reason, people never lived on the ground floor of such houses. When a generator was installed and the house was wired for electricity, certain parts of it became electrified, particularly the damp floor of its entrance. Before the problem was overcome, visitors would sometimes be caused to leap and hop the last few yards to the staircase!

"All's well" and shark oil

One of the advantages of living in a town the size of Dubai was that I was brought into contact with most aspects of its varied life. In size it combined all the advantages of a village, being small enough to enable one to be conversant with all that was happening, but sufficiently large to avoid being parochial.

It was a cosmopolitan town in which it was impossible to live without being aware of the dual importance of its position, seaward to the great maritime trading area reached by its sailing fleet, and landward to the vast expanses of the whole of south-eastern Arabia. Just as Dubai had its own very special features and character, it

Right. A well-known personality in Dubai, Khalifa bin Mohammed, also known as Al Akraf which means "the lame one". Note the iron bars across the glassless window behind him, and the shutters and doors made from imported wood.

Below. Windtowers were an effective means of cooling before the advent of air-conditioning.

also had its own distinctive sounds and smells. They are but some of the aspects of its life that cannot be conveyed in an album, yet they remain in my memory as clearly as its images are depicted in the photographs. A blind beggar once told me that he could find his way around Dubai merely by listening to its many sounds. Only now does it occur to me that one could have been similarly guided by its smells, some pleasant, others less so, their intensity constantly changing according to the amount of humidity in the air.

Bedu visiting Dubai would tether their camels and leave them as close as possible to the suq, ready to load with any supplies they bought. The tract of sand around our house was a popular spot for this purpose, and my wife and I grew accustomed to their many different noises. They seemed to have a grunt or a groan for every occasion, varying the volume according to the degree of their protest, the loudest being when they were being loaded with heavy sacks and filled water skins. Even when at rest, they seemed to keep up a fairly continuous commentary to each other, never more than when a bull camel was provoking them with his bellowing. During the heat of a summer's afternoon they were at their quietest, but even then their digestive processes kept them gurgling and singing at both ends, as Saif the poet described it. Surprisingly, we could not smell their presence, even when close, although their breath sometimes left something to be desired.

No sound the camel was capable of producing could compete with the braying of a donkey, and that was to be heard with some frequency. But there was one sound similarly produced by both beasts: the succulent noise of them crunching and grinding date stones given to them as a treat.

Many of Dubai's sounds and smells emanated from the creek and all the activity that took place on and around its shores. During the day they tended to combine into one, but at other times they were more distinct. At night the single splash of any object thrown into the water could be clearly heard, as could the creaking of the abra-man's boat as he rowed through the darkness with fluorescence dripping from his oars.

A strong gust of wind would sweep all smells before it and cause vessels to bump into each other with loud bangs as teak hit teak, invariably followed by a chorus of shouts from their awakened crews. Riggings flapped and fluttered ceaselessly during a wind, and if not removed a single awning could vibrate and resound annoyingly the whole night long. Boatmen hailed each other, and sometimes a crew would sit on deck under a swinging hurricane lamp, singing or chanting to the rhythm of a drum. But that would subside as the town fell silent, which was their cue to take their own rest.

Right. Saif bin Khalfan bel Jafla. A bedu of some repute who once shot-up a caravan single-handed; a pearl diver who, like many, went blind towards the end of his life; he was also known as Saif the poet, despite being illiterate.

Below. An abra-man rowing across the creek. The fare depended on the number of people travelling together in a boat.

It was during a dead calm, when the air was motionless, that odours were most noticeable, particularly when they merged with a mist to hang heavily over the town. The worst odours were from large quantities of dried sprats (oumer) which had been amassed by merchants ready for export. Their pungency made them a very unpopular cargo with the crews of the ships that would carry them away to be made into fertiliser used by distant gardeners and farmers. Another unpleasant stench came from shark and other fish oil used for preserving the timbers of vessels which were pulled over on their beams or beached for maintenance, Pleasanter aromas sometimes emerged from the unpleasant, and were welcome. One evening when the smell of fish predominated, a large Indian sailing vessel moored nearby became enveloped in a cloud of smoke as its crew prepared their evening meal. The smoke wafted over to us, carrying with it such a tempting aroma of curry, that my wife and I changed our minds about what to have for supper, and had curried safi (our favourite fish) instead of the dish we had planned. Then followed the clattering of dishes as two of the crew squatted on the shore scouring them with sand.

After the advent of electricity, the usual daytime background noise in "Bait Bamela", as our little house (or, rather, Pamela's House) became known, was the pulsating of a ceiling fan, but in late afternoon or early evening that was often drowned out by the throbbing of drums and the rhythm of Baluchi pipes as professional entertainers who lived nearby got into their stride to attend weddings or circumcision ceremonies. Sometimes they would continue the music late into the night for their own pleasure.

Considering that Dubai had no sewage system or toilets (other than the pits dug in a few private houses) and the majority of people performed their acts of nature in the open, the town was remarkably free of those sorts of unpleasant smells. Several factors combined to achieve this, with the sea, tides, sand, sun and fish being the natural carers of the environment. Most relevant of all was the personal hygiene and commonsense of the population. Anyone using the creek would get close to the waterline so that the movement of the water would clear their deposits and enable the creek's dense population of fish to complete the cleaning-up process, as with the waste from the little, open toilet boxes suspended from the sides of the vessels. For that reason, although easy to catch, fish from the creek were never eaten and were only used when needed as bait. Those who used the sands around the town for their toiletry had simply to cover over their debris with sand. Salt water and intense sun were great purifiers. For the individual, there was nothing better than the code of hygiene taught by Islam, to which there was strict adherence. One could sit and eat with any bedu without qualms about his personal

Right. Instruments of African origin were often played by entertainers at celebrations.

Below. A jelbut beached for maintenance on the shores of the creek near Bury Khalifa.

cleanliness, even though he might be travel-worn and his only shirt threadbare and dirty.

Of pleasanter things, our house would often smell of rose water and frankincense after we had visitors, particularly during the days of the eid (religious holiday) when the whole town would be pervaded with their aromas. Although these adjuncts of hospitality were something of a formality for many townees, they had real meaning to a traveller. After a long journey or period spent out in the sands, to arrive at someone's hut or open encampment, and to receive whatever hospitality was within the means of the host, was a great joy. If thirsty, the traveller would first be given water, then coffee with light refreshments (fuwala), for even if invited to a meal, the preparation of it, starting with the dhabiha (the killing of a goat or chicken), would take some time. Before the guest departed, rose water was sprinkled over his head and he would be handed the awd (frankincense) gently burning in a small terracotta container. Each person seemed to have his own way of enjoying the fragrant smoke. Some would hold it under their beards whilst fastidiously combing them out with their fingers, some would hold it under their cloaks, whilst the connoisseur would pull a cloak over his head and disappear with the awd inside his improvised tent.

A reasonable level of security was maintained in Dubai territory, due largely to the reputation and success of its shaikhs in catching miscreants. Even so, there was still some risk of attack and, up to the early 1950's, raiding parties from afar would sometimes swoop on the outskirts of Dubai and swiftly make off with their spoils. So the watchtowers around the town were constantly manned, their sentinels loudly calling out to each other with a deeply guttural, "All's well," throughout the night.

Without any doubt, the loveliest, and least frequent, sound was that of young voices singing as they moved about the town. As they approached, their refrain became clearer. Decked in colourful new clothes and laden with gold jewellery, one of the group of young girls accompanied by their teacher (sometimes, but not always, including a young boy or two) would shrilly chant a short verse from the Koran. At the end of the verse, all would lustily join in the singing of a loud amen, the word from which the name, "tawmina", of their little graduation ceremony derived.

For sheer variety, nothing could compete with the cacophony of sounds and the fusion of smells to be found in the suq, from the tinsmith's hammer to the cries of vendors, and from heady spices to eastern perfumes. That, most of all, was where my senses were engraved with indelible memories of the sounds and aromas of old Dubai.

Right. Yusif Mirza, in charge of his father's shop. Nothing could compete with the cacophony of sounds and the fusion of smells to be found in the suq.

Below. A young lady of a tawmina.

From right to left: Shaikh Rashid bin Saeed Al Maktoum, Hamad Al Futtaim and Saif bin Kalban.

Waterfront scene on the curve of the creek where Shindaga was separated from Dubai.

DUBAI
AT
MID-CENTURY

DIARY EXTRACT: 5th April 1948

❝ I first arrived in Dubai accompanied by Kevin Harrison, a bearded R.A.F. chaplain with whom I had managed to get the use of a Bedford truck to drive here from Sharjah. (The few lorries in use locally, operating mainly between Sharjah and Dubai, were mostly Bedford trucks disposed of by the R.A.F. They became so well-known that "Bidfod" was absorbed into Arabic as the word for lorry.) Only a short distance from Sharjah we ran into a problem in a salt marsh known in Arabic as a sabkha. The stuff seemed worse than mud, but with a chuckled invocation to the Almighty from Kevin, we soon extricated ourselves. It was not long before we were travelling on soft, white sand between scattered date palms and houses made from their fronds, on the outskirts of a part of Dubai known as Deira. Following the tracks near to the shore of a large, salt-water inlet, we entered the town through a shaded suq where merchants sat in the dark recesses of small, open-fronted booths, and which was so narrow that at one point a loaded donkey had to be pushed halfway into one of the booths to allow us to pass. Within a few hundred yards the truck could go no further, and we continued on foot to where an open space between the booths served as a landing stage for the many small boats that provided a ferry service across the wide creek. Rowed by a single oarsman with crudely shaped oars tied to the sides of the boat, they were Dubai's "gondolas".

We crossed the inlet to Dubai on the opposite bank. I assume that it is the oldest part as it has given its name to the whole town, as well as to the port and to the entire Shaikhdom. A third sector of the town called Shindaga only came into view after we had crossed the creek. It was built on a low-lying spit of land that extended to the creek's entrance.

The wide variety of costumes seen in Deira is an indication of its role as a cosmopolitan trading centre, but in Dubai I felt I was in Arabia. Bedu tribesmen wearing curved daggers and bandoliers of ammunition tugged their protesting camels into the narrow alleyways of the suq, presumably having arrived from the interior to buy supplies. We walked to the fringes of the town and waded across a flooded flat to reach Shindaga. There we hailed a ferryboat back to Deira, but the boatman had to row very hard across the current flowing out to sea. Only by following the shoreline in Deira were we able to find our way back to our "Bidfod".

I have fallen for Dubai's bazaars — in fact, for Dubai. ❞

Right. A cloth merchant in Deira suq writing a letter for his customer who is sitting on the foldable extension to the booth.

Below. The main abra landing stage at Deira was called "Bank Landing" as the building shown was the only bank on the Trucial Coast. It opened in 1946 as the Imperial Bank of Iran but later changed its name to the British Bank of the Middle East.

Many of the craftsmen in the suq had no shop, but worked on a vacant piece of ground as close as possible to their clients. They were known by name, and the cry would go round the suq, "Where is Hassan the mattress-maker?" until it reached him and he was able to make contact with the potential client. A mattress-maker's creation was vulnerable to visits from passers-by, who might stop to pray on it or simply to rest and chat. Seeing a shaikh sitting on the mattress below, one of his subjects took the opportunity to stop and seek his advice.

Other suq traders, like the baker on the right, had their own little shops or booths. At night they were lit by hurricane lamps which the shopkeepers later used to light their way home.

DIARY EXTRACT: 15th April 1948

❝ Met for the first time the Ruler of Dubai (Shaikh Saeed bin Maktoum) and his son Rashid when I called on them to thank them for the camels and escort they had provided for my trip from Dubai to the Dhaid area.

Grey-haired and walking with the aid of a stick, Shaikh Saeed must be over sixty (in fact, he was born in 1878), although he is of slight build and is a good-looking man with very clear eyes. Shaikh Rashid is in his thirties, with black hair, very large, flashing eyes and quick movements. They were very friendly, patient with my attempts at Arabic and amused at its Egyptian/Lebanese mix. They were further amused when I said that I was Codrai bin Codrai, for to have the same name for son and father is to indicate not knowing one's father!

They served refreshments consisting of dates, vermicelli sprinkled with sugar, and tinned peach slices. Chasing and trying to grasp the peaches with the fingers calls for a special skill (which I did not possess but later acquired). After coffee, a container of burning frankincense was passed round the majlis, but had been over-fuelled and gave off clouds of smoke which filled the room and caused some of the large assembly to cough. On the Ruler's instructions it was placed outside the door. When I left, a camel squatting near the door was bellowing furiously, either at the smoke or because it was being branded.

The Ruler's house is practical for receiving the many townees and bedu who seem to call on him, and the only furnishings in his majlis are carpets. ❞

Right. Shaikh Saeed bin Maktoum.

Below. Shaikh Rashid bin Saeed Al Maktoum.

Aerial view of the tip of Deira, adjacent to the entrance to the creek, with Sharjah in the distant background.

A bra's were a notable feature of life, being the main means of crossing the creek between the three sections of town, and of transporting people to vessels anchored away from the shores of the creek. In summer, the abra men tied awnings over their craft to shade their passengers from the sun, but they had to be removed when a strong wind was blowing as, even without them, it required strong pulling on the oars to row the abras across the strong tidal currents.

The abras would stop anywhere, but the picture on the right shows one of the main landing stages on the Dubai side, often used by people wishing to share a boat with others to cross to Deira. This is the first photograph I ever took of Dubai, in 1948.

Below, the Ruler of Ajman, Shaikh Rashid bin Humaid Al Naimi, crossing the creek while on a visit to Dubai.

Public celebrations on the fringe of Dubai.

DIARY EXTRACT: 15th May 1948

❝ My first arrival in Dubai by sea — on the "Fat Al Khair". Good to be ashore. Met Wilfred Thesiger who has just arrived from Sharjah where he had been staying for a couple of days after his second crossing of the Empty Quarter. Jacko Jackson (Representative of the oil company for which Bird works) is kindly putting us both up. He seems to be a very good Arabist, very knowledgeable about local affairs — and very tolerant of people who arrive dressed only in a wazar! A coincidence that two of the very few Ingleez in the region are both "Jackson" (Noel Jackson was the Political Officer in Sharjah).

Could have listened all night to Thesiger's account of his travels. I told him that when news of his first crossing of the Empty Quarter appeared in The Times, I was with Bertram Thomas (the first to cross the Empty Quarter in 1931, a short time before St.John Philby made his crossing) and he had commented that nowadays explorers had all sorts of modern aids such as radios. Thought at first that Thesiger was not amused, but he grinned broadly, for he had had no advantage over Thomas who, he said, tried to run an "Officers' Mess" and did not always eat with his companions. ❞

Of the three men whose names will forever remain linked with the exploration of the Empty Quarter:-

Bertram Thomas visited Abu Dhabi a few months later, after ceasing to be the Director of Studies at the Middle East Centre for Arab Studies, and joining Shell. He was not well, and died where he was born, near Bristol, on Ist January 1951.

St.John Philby died in Beirut on Ist October 1960.

Wilfred Thesiger is now in his 82nd year and periodically visits the United Arab Emirates and the Sultanate of Oman.

Right. A jelbut under sail, with Dubai's skyline in the background.

Below. Wilfred Thesiger in May 1948 after his second crossing of the Empty Quarter.

This group of trees in the south-eastern part of Dubai territory was a popular camping site for bedu and hunting parties.

As soon as bedu stopped and kindled a fire, that particular spot in the desert became a centre which others in the vicinity would visit. News was exchanged and coffee and food shared with the visitors. Meat (usually goat or chicken, but sometimes young camels or wild game) was a luxury, and not eaten regularly. The killing of a goat was a special event — a feast — but such was the strong tradition of hospitality in the desert that, after a meal had been prepared, anyone who arrived at the encampment had to be invited to share it. Around prayer-time, each prayed individually, afterwards rising to greet the others according to the time of day.

Note the European jackets which had become very popular among the bedu in winter. They were imported secondhand and sold in the suqs of the coast, some of them being ex-uniform jackets.

DIARY EXTRACT: 3rd April 1949

66 Another visit to Ras Al Khaimah, where the Ruler is still having problems with some of his dissident tribal leaders. I took the opportunity to visit Shaikh Rashid at his father's date garden at Shemal, a very pleasant retreat for him and his family. There is a small, mud-brick house among the palms which is little used other than as a shelter during bad weather. Otherwise it is given over to the drying of home-grown tobacco which keeps all the family supplied for the tiny, "one-minute" pipes which are smoked by nearly all the Dubai shaikhs. When dry, the tobacco is rubbed into a fine and very dry, green flaky mixture which is kept in a small tin or leather pouch and tipped into the pipe. 99

Smokers often kept their pipes tucked in the cords around their headcloths, and it was not unusual for anyone wanting a smoke to borrow it, as I found when I smoked an English pipe and it too was taken and passed around the majlis. I tried Rashid's tobacco in my pipe but it was not a success as it was so fine that it was difficult to draw through a large bowl of it, and it sometimes gave rise to a miniature pyrotechnic display.

Right. The tiny pipes were smoked mainly by people of tribal origin, including the shaikhs.

Below. Tobacco grown and dried in Ras Al Khaimah and Fujairah is here being sold in Dubai suq.

*S*haikh Juma bin Maktoum (born 1891) and,
below, Shaikh Hasher bin Maktoum (born 1899),
were both brothers of Shaikh Saeed bin Maktoum,
Ruler of Dubai from 1912 to 1958.

DIARY EXTRACT: 20th April 1949

❝A messenger arrived this morning from Shaikh Saeed to say that he was encamped in the desert some twenty-odd miles south of Dubai, and would Thesiger (who was staying with me after his 1948/9 crossing of the Empty Quarter), Bird and I like to join him for dinner. We accepted the invitation, and the messenger hurried off to the Ruler's home in Shindaga to collect carpets and large cooking pots. Shortly afterwards I heard a shot ring out and I saw a group of armed tribesmen leaving town in a hurry. Wrongly, I supposed that this had some bizarre connection with dinner. It was not until later, when there was an outbreak of celebratory firing from the returning warriors, that I learned they had rushed to Shaikh Saeed's assistance on hearing a rumour, which proved false, that he was under attack.

Thesiger, Bird and I enjoyed a lantern-lit spread with Saeed and his sons, as did a large number of bedu who ate in quorums until the food was finished. They had been drawn to the feast from the surrounding desert, just as every flying insect in Arabia seemed to have been attracted by the light of the lanterns. ❞

Armed tribesmen enjoying a camp fire, right, and protecting Shaikh Saeed, below.

With anchors dropped or mooring ropes secured, small, crowded pearling vessels came to rest in their home ports. For their crews, after a strenuous season of hardship and privation, the joy of homecoming and reunion with families was heightened or tempered by the size of the season's catch and its financial outcome. Finally, hulls had to be scraped and oiled, and the vessels cleaned and repaired before they were either laid-up for the winter or put into other service.

DIARY EXTRACT: 24th October 1949

66 The last of Dubai's pearling boats arrived back in port today, but their crews seemed to be chanting with less gusto than usual as it has not been a good season. This, and the declining world market for pearls, gives no comfort to Dubai's merchants who are becoming increasingly concerned at a prolonged slump in trade.

They have recently sent a deputation to the Ruler requesting him to increase pressure on the (oil) company to step-up its operations.

Ghanim told me that a strong party of Dubai bedu had given chase and recovered camels stolen during a raid on them near Buraimi. 99

Right. A pearling boat returning to Dubai at the end of the season.

Below. Ghanim bin Ali, a close friend of the author. Sand on the nose and forehead, a result of praying in the desert, was a common sight.

Children would clamber aboard the anchored pearling vessels to greet their relatives when they returned at the end of the season.

DIARY EXTRACT: 14th February 1950

❝Stories of the toll exacted by yesterday's storm are beginning to circulate. A boom carrying sixty passengers from Dubai is reported missing, as well as several jelbuts, and I saw a Bahraini craft which had been wrecked on the shores of Jumaira with a loss of eleven lives. Its nakhuda was standing despairingly on what remained of its broken poop, surrounded by a skeleton of teak ribs. Could he have been wondering whether a barren woman had slept on its newly laid keel and subsequently conceived (a folk tale that the life of one of the vessel's crew would be forfeit for any new life thus created)? The total count of lives lost in the region will never be known, as no record is kept of the losses other than in the memories of grieving relatives.❞

Many lives were lost every year in shipwrecks but at the time there was no news media to record such tragedies.

After the afternoon (asr) prayers, a small group of performers would move through town to an open space on its fringe — announcing their whereabouts with the loud beating of a drum to rouse the populace. Arriving at the chosen site, they would stick a flagpole in the ground to provide a rallying point for any who chose to join in. As people left their houses and arrived at the celebrations, they would join one of the several groups that were forming. Those of tribal origin would join a group of solemn dancers slowly moving in dignified movement with their rifles held aloft, crying out their tribal rallying call. They would acknowledge the presence of their shaikh by the occasional, one-handed firing of a rifle. The professional entertainers provided the main and noisiest impetus to the proceedings. Some joined groups in which instruments of African origin were played. Exuberant sword dancers were at the centre of other groups. Ladies modestly retired a short distance from the other dancers to perform their own dance, the noban.

DIARY EXTRACT:
20th March 1950

"Wilfred Thesiger, accompanied by Salim bin Kabina (right) and Salim bin Ghubaisha, arrived in Dubai today after their journey through Oman."

A flagpole being erected by a small group of performers at a site chosen for public celebrations.

DIARY EXTRACT: 24th May 1950

66 A wounded Rashidi, called Mubarak, was brought to Dubai by Salim bin Ghubaisha, for medical treatment. It appears that five members of the Al Rashid tribe, two of them ex-Thesiger's party, had shot up a group of Bani Ali near Ramlat Annaij. One of the Bani Ali had been killed and another injured, which will further worsen relations between the two tribes. Mubarak, an uncomplaining and very pleasant person, had his wound cleaned and his arm put in a sling, but nothing further can be done for him in Dubai as the bullet has lodged in a bone and an X-ray and operation are necessary. The northbound mail steamer (Maaley) will be leaving in a couple of days for Bahrain, where he can be treated, although he has made it clear that he will not go there without Salim. If they go, it will be their first journey by sea. 99

Mubarak with his arm in a sling and, below, with bin Ghubaisha and another Rashidi.

The mariners of the Gulf, inheritors of a long seafaring tradition, were the aristocrats of the sea, just as the bedu were the aristocrats of the sands. They carried out their tasks with the minimum of orders from the nakhuda (captain), instinctively knowing what had to be done and what was expected of them. Fearlessly, they regarded the climbing of a mast or into the sometimes precarious riggings as being no more than the climbing of a palm tree. Such accidents as did occur were most likely to be caused by worn riggings; and repairing the hull, sails and riggings was a constant task.

A car load of cheering supporters spurring on their favourite camel.

DIARY EXTRACT: 28th August 1951

❝ Mail arrived on the Sanaan (the south bound B.I. steamer) this morning. I had just settled down to read the newspapers after lunch when the quiet of the afternoon was broken by gun fire. It came from the guards in the watchtowers who had spotted smoke rising from the area of barasti huts adjacent to my house and who were competing with each other in firing off their old ammunition (for which they would later seek reimbursement from the Shaikh) to prove their wakefulness in sounding the alarm and in rousing the people. Fire was a very serious matter, for unless quickly controlled it could spread through the tinder-dry barasti huts at an alarming speed, placing the whole town at risk within minutes. Then I remembered our new fire extinguishers. I roused the staff and we rushed the heavy extinguishers to the nearby scene of the fire, where everyone stopped their frantic fire-fighting activity to make way for us. Were the strange objects we carried to be their salvation? Durub was the first to get an extinguisher working but, not knowing what to expect, was hit in the face by its jet. But it soon became apparent that the limited contents of half-a-dozen extinguishers would have little impact on the fire, though they did give rise to some short-lived hilarity when Sabir sprayed Rihan who immediately retaliated, which led to everyone being fairly well sprayed. The Knights who had rushed to the rescue with their Western magic, pulled back ignominiously with their empty, red cylinders, and the hut owners and fast-increasing number of helpers resumed their frantic efforts. It was interesting to observe their much-practised, simple and effective way of fire fighting. A wet rope was thrown across a burning hut and its walls of burning, dry palm fronds pulled to the ground, allowing anyone trapped inside the hut to escape. Once the burning mass was on the ground, the fire fighters closed in on it from windward, rapidly scooping soft sand over it as they moved, and the fire was soon under control. The outcome would have been different had there been fewer people to fight the blaze — or if the guards in the watchtowers had not been so alert. ❞

Most of the barasti fires were caused by a spark blown from an open fire or by an accident with a primus stove, but were often followed by gossip to the effect that it had been started during a domestic quarrel. The contents of a hut were laid bare by a fire, in some instances revealing articles that ought not to have been there!

Right and below. The traditional method of fire fighting.

Most of a crew's catch of pearls would not be sold until they returned to port at the end of the pearling season, but some would be sold to the "tawash", the floating pearl merchants who visited the pearling banks on their own vessels, seeking whatever opportunities there were for buying pearls. Such merchants would spread carpets over the poop deck which would become their offices, keeping their measuring and grading paraphernalia, as well as the pearls, in heavy Kuwaiti-type chests.

Right. A well-known pearl broker, Mohammed Saeed Al Mahmud, on a visit to a gold dealer in Dubai.

Below. The "tawash" would carefully inspect the pearls before negotiating a price with the captain of the vessel.

DIARY EXTRACT: 25th March 1952

❝ A Dubai merchant recently passed-off four lacs of Rupees (a lac equals a hundred thousand rupees) worth of cultured pearls as being genuine, natural pearls before his fraud was discovered. The Ruler is naturally greatly concerned in case this should dishonour all Trucial Coast merchants and ruin the pearl trade. It is understood that the same merchant did something similar in Bahrain a few years ago, though on a smaller scale. He has now been prohibited from further dealings and, after representations from the Rulers of Sharjah and Ajman, it has been agreed to appoint someone to introduce a system of inspecting pearls sold in Dubai and to test for cultured ones.

It is being claimed that three camels have been killed by poisoned bait spread in Dubai territory to kill locusts. Whether or not this is true, it will certainly make it more difficult for the Rulers to agree to the use of such bait. ❞

Right. A pearl diver rests for a short time between dives, by clinging to a rope draped over an oar. Wearing a bone or wooden clip over his nostrils, a good diver could stay down for over two minutes even in very deep water. He would continue diving for up to an hour before taking a rest in the boat.

Below. Sorting, grading, weighing and valuing pearls.

A large sambuq at anchor in Dubai creek.

DIARY EXTRACT: 3rd April 1952

❝ A memorable but exhausting day yesterday. Left Bahrain for Sharjah on the last stage of our journey to Dubai. After our marriage on 26th February, we had travelled to Cyprus, Lebanon and Iraq where our honeymoon was extended by a signal from London asking me to photograph and write an article about the excavations at Nimrod and Ninevah being conducted under the leadership of Max Mallowan and his wife (Agatha Christie).

An early departure from Bahrain on an Anson. I made the same mistake as always of accepting an invitation to sit in "the office", the price of which was to have to wind-up the undercarriage — 87 turns! On arrival in Sharjah, Pamela and I slid down the wing of the Anson to be greeted by a large number of people who had very kindly turned out to welcome us. Biggest surprise of all was the sight of a large, open, convertible Studebaker, flying Dubai's flag, which I was told Shaikh Rashid had just bought and had now sent to meet us. As soon as we reached Dubai we were greeted with rifle fire by Ghanim and others waiting for us outside our new house, and by the singing of a group of children in their best bibs and tuckers. Then followed a constant stream of visitors led by Shaikhs Saeed, Rashid, Juma, Khalifa and Hashar. A very touching and sincere welcome home by a family that had been so kind to me during my bachelor days. Pamela excelled herself with some resounding, practised "Salaam Alaikums", but her few words of newly acquired Arabic did not go far when she was visited by a group of ladies. Presents of carpets and coffee pots arrived from the shaikhs. Tonight Shaikhs Saeed and Rashid invited me over for dinner.

Was greatly relieved to find that Pamela approved of our little home which has already become known as "Bait Bamela". In fact she was pleasantly surprised and relieved to find it somewhat better than my description. However, I feared the worst when she let out a scream on entering the bathroom. (With Rihan's help I had organised this appendage to the house. On stone supports, it had purposely been built without windows so that it could also be used as a darkroom. Although it was rather Spartan-looking it was very practical and ahead of its time for Dubai, and I was proud of it.) For a moment I sensed an impending divorce, but all was well! Someone had given us a present of a dhabb (large, spiny-tailed lizard) which had been left in the bathroom, where the poor, scared creature sat puffing with fright and sticking out its black tongue at Pamela!

Exhausted but very happy when we turned in, deeply touched by the warmth and kindness of our welcome. ❞

Right. The author and his wife with some of the children who greeted them on their arrival in Dubai after their marriage:

Below. A spiny-tailed lizard known as a dhabb.

Shindaga. A shelter of palm fronds has been made over the poop deck of a jelbut while it undergoes repairs.

Swarm of locusts over Dubai.

DIARY EXTRACT: 28th February 1953

66 A unexpected visit from Shaikh Rashid today who surprised me with a present — a British sailor who had been found wandering on a track around Dubai creek. He told me that he had deserted from the "Wild Goose" (a British sloop anchored off Dubai), and had hoped to get a lift on a local craft to Bombay. I couldn't make up my mind whether to admire and sympathise with him for his search for adventure or whether to have harsh thoughts of him for his disloyalty. Later, three naval patrolmen came to escort him back to his ship. Rashid was greatly amused by the incident and curious to know what might happen to the sailor. So was I.

Awakened at 4 a.m. by a very strong shamal — rain, hail and lightning. Very dramatic. Spent the rest of the night mopping up the water that had dripped through the roof or been blown in through the cracks in the shutters. Many barastis blown down. Three vessels blown away from their moorings caused damage as they were blown up the creek, crashing into other vessels. 99

Right. The "Wild Goose" anchored off Shindaga, the closest safe anchorage near to the shore. Local craft usually did the ferrying between ship and shore over the hazardous bar at the entrance to the creek, for which local expertise was vital.

Below. Barastis such as these were often damaged or destroyed in bad storms.

Aerial view from the north of the eastern extremity of Deira, taken in 1951.

DIARY EXTRACT: 17th September 1953

❝ I had just loaded the first of my Liwa films into the tank and poured in the developer when Shaikh Rashid, Khalifa bin Mohammed and Abdulla bin Husain arrived. They were very amused that I had to sit in the majlis agitating the tank whilst looking at the timer, then dash off to discharge its contents and pour in the fixer. The reason for their unexpected visit was to congratulate me on my trip to the Liwa and on my narrow escape from death which they had just learnt about. (This is the subject of extracts from my diaries which appear in the volume on Abu Dhabi).

I was deeply touched by their friendly and sincere concern for me, although Pamela was shocked as this was the first she had heard of my mishap. They were all most interested in my trip, Khalifa in particular when it came to place names, for a few years before he had led a large raiding party on an attack there from Dubai. They remained for some time, so that after a few brief absences I was able to show them my film hanging up to dry.

Rashid brought his shy little daughter Hassa with him. She took to Pamela who admired her pigtails and her gold necklace. ❞

Right. Khalifa bin Mohammed, known as Al Akraf or "the lame one", was a trusted companion of Shaikhs Saeed and Rashid. He was renowned for the attack he led on the Bani Yas in the Liwa.

Below. Abdulla bin Husain, also a close companion of the Ruler of Dubai.

Shaikh Rashid, left, on the outskirts of Dubai, with a
falconing party which included, from right to left, Saif bin
Nasser, Ahmed Al Bawardi and Obaid bin Ghanam.

DIARY EXTRACT: 31st October 1953

❝ The falconing season has begun, and the price of falcons (particularly those brought from Persia) is soaring. Shaikh Rashid bought a bird today for fifteen hundred Rupees which is said to be a new record price here, though far higher prices have been paid in Saudi Arabia.

Boats have returned from the pearling banks and, although the trade in pearls continues to decline, good profits are reported to have been made this year as a result of a reduced number of pearls being marketed by fewer people. One diver has a badly injured hand caused by an attack by a barracuda on the banks off-shore from Jebel Ali. ❞

Right. Pearl divers shared the sea with sharks, sea snakes, barracuda and large jellyfish which could infict a painful sting, causing a fever which lasted for several days. When there were shoals of them about, divers wore one-piece cotton garments for protection.

Below. A falcon in flight.

Once a member of a shaikh's retinue had been charged with the training and care of a newly aquired falcon, it became his constant companion. Becoming accustomed to people and to life at ground level was an important part of the bird's training. If it took fright, its handler immediately soothed it or donned its hood. The bird on the right had been in captivity for some time, and remained undisturbed by the glitter and activity of this party of girls. Below, is a young falconer with a bird given to him by his father. To those who were interested and who grew up in the families or retinues of the shaikhs, the art of falconry was naturally acquired. It was the sport of shaikhs, and any falcons caught by the bedu would be taken to the shaikhs in return for a reward. Wealthy merchants who could afford the sport were not usually interested in it and did not feel secure venturing into the desert.

Most of the population were illiterate which did not mean that they were ignorant; indeed, some were poets and most were masters of rhetoric. The written word was respected in that it was the language of the Koran, but in practical matters many distrusted it because it put them at a disadvantage.

On the few occasions when there had to be recourse to the written word, "professional" scribes were employed for a small fee, although literate shopkeepers and merchants would often oblige their customers with this task. In the few places where opportunities existed, mostly in towns and villages, children learned to read and write in Koran classes. Others slavishly copied lessons given to them by well-wishers. Mohammed bin Ghanim, right, is here seen frowning in concentration.

Shaikh Khalifa bin Saeed Al Maktoum assessing and selecting good riding camels.

Throughout Dubai territory, every drop of
sweet water had to be hauled to the surface from
man-dug wells.

Desert wells were of different types, varying from
the unlined wells for travellers which usually had to
be cleared before use, to this cement-lined well at
Nakhara which was kept in constant use. Camels
and goat herds were brought to the well for
watering, converging on it from many directions,
and goat skins were filled and carried away on
donkeys for domestic use. It was hard work that
had to be done swiftly to make way for the next
users. There was much chatter and exchanging of
news, and the water was hauled from the well to
the rhythm of a chant.

DIARY EXTRACT: 6th May 1954

66 Found an elderly man slumped at the doorway, frail, trembling and clearly very ill, probably suffering from malaria. He wore a Persian style headcloth and was not a beggar. I gave him some medicine and told Ibrahim and Hamza to look after him and give him further medicine. 99

DIARY EXTRACT: 14th May 1954

66 Arrived home to find the sick man whom I had found at the door a week or so ago waiting for me. He still looked frail but much better than when I had last seen him. Very politely and in faltering Arabic he said that he had come to thank me, so Pamela invited him in to have tea with us. After noisily sucking his tea with great relish he said that he had heard of my interest in his people, who turned out to be those who performed the "mureed". He then unfurled a cloth covering a long bundle and pulled out of it a stiletto. Without further ado, he pulled back his shirt and pushed it through his rather scraggy shoulder. There it stayed, protruding from him as Pamela passed him some biscuits and we finished tea. He did not bleed. 99

Right and below. A stiletto being used in a mureed ceremony.

Literally, "mureed" means "one who is desirous or willing". The ceremony began with the warming of drums, and when the skins were tight they were beaten in slow tempo to accompany those who loudly chanted "Allah", as they performed a series of gyrations with their arms and bodies. This lasted for some time, and when the participants eventually rose and formed themselves into a circle they appeared to be in a hypnotic state. One by one, their leader then summoned participants to the centre of the circle to have a stiletto tapped through their shoulders, or to be handed a naked sword with which to beat their backs or bellies.

A mureed ceremony.

DIARY EXTRACT: 16th November 1954

"Abdulla bin Husain called to show us a new falcon which Shaikh Rashid had brought while he was travelling. I opened my tripod in the sitting room so that the bird could perch on its horizontal handle whilst we were having tea. Abdulla removed its hood and, after a bit of fluttering and decorating of our carpet, it settled down and spent the whole time blinking its eyes as it appraised the scene. Wonder what he made of us all and his first English tea party."

Falcons, a guest sticking a stiletto through himself, another pulling snakes out of his shirt, children bringing us shells, an injured curlew and other birds, a dhabb sticking out his black tongue at us, were just some of the accompaniments to tea in our little majlis.

During the training and hunting season, a frequent sight was that of a falconer with a falcon on his cuff. He was seldom separated from his bird, which he carried with him everywhere, allowing it to become familiar with everyday sights and sounds. The falcon became accustomed to its handler who, in turn, became acquainted with the bird's special characteristics, and a remarkable bond of understanding developed between them.

This falconer, Humaid bin Amhai, was a trusted retainer to Shaikh Rashid and was assigned to pass on his falconry skills to Shaikh Mohammed bin Rashid.

DIARY EXTRACT: 23rd March 1955

66 Farewell Dubai!

Feeling extremely sad. Difficult to explain to Rashid and other friends that I am not leaving from choice, and they make my departure feel like a breach of friendship.

In sha Allah I will return, although I feel that life here as I have known it will not stay the same for very much longer. Already there are many signs of change. 99

Water donkeys carrying sweet water from the wells of Jumaira, seen crossing Ghubaiba at high tide.

"*Reflections*"

AL AKUS

Around the middle of this century a camera was still a rare sight in south-eastern Arabia and, when I photographed them, many of my subjects were seeing one for the first time. Imaginatively, both camera and photographs were aptly referred to as "al akus", meaning "reflections".

Considering the extent to which people in the region had been isolated from such modern innovations, they were exceedingly tolerant of the strange object pointed in their direction. In part, this may have been due to the fact that I always tried to maintain an acceptable standard of etiquette when photographing, without which the camera can be an unwelcome intrusion into privacy. As far as circumstances would permit, and without too much loss of spontaneity, I either sought permission before photographing, or tried to get my subjects interested in what I was doing by letting them look through the camera's viewfinder — a novel and amusing experience for most. Due largely to the good nature of the people I was photographing or travelling with, my photographic endeavours have invariably been shared experiences, pleasurable to me and entertaining to others.

Whenever possible, I later showed the results to those I photographed but, on the whole, my subjects were usually more interested in obtaining one of my screw-top film canisters in which to keep finely chopped local tobacco for their tiny pipes, than they were in the photographs. More photographs resulted in more canisters and so photography was popular!

During the early post-war years there was a dearth of photographic equipment on the market, and most cameras were expensive and of a pre-war vintage. When I went to the Trucial Coast, it was with a Cirroflex (a fairly cheap American copy of the Rolleiflex) bought in Egypt in 1946. Later, I acquired a large antique Thornton Pickard quarter-plate reflex camera, beautifully made and with a superb Cooke lens in a large brass mount. It was a joy to play with, but as plates were hard to find I obtained a large roll-film adaptor which was a disaster as it scratched tramlines on the whole length of the film. Had I kept that camera, it would today be a valuable collectors' item. Instead, I disposed of it to someone who, I was later told, preferred it for its size and potential use for gold smuggling!

On a later visit to Bahrain, I treated myself to a newly arrived, post-war Rolleiflex; a quality camera of which my Cirroflex was but a poor imitation. The Rolleiflex has been used by many of the masters of photography since it came into being in the early 1930's, its main photographic limitations being a relatively wide-angle,

Haji Ghulam, who looked after the author's transport fleet, being "framed" for a photograph.